Alaska

T0107086

Barrow

Fairbanks

▲ Denali

Nome

Anchorage

Juneau

Homer

Gulf of Alaska

Bering Sea

Aleutian Islands

Pacific Ocean

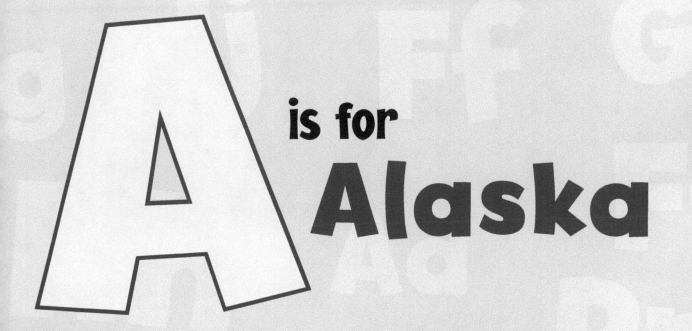

A is for Alaska

**written by kids
for kids**

WESTWINDS
PRESS®

A
is for **Anchorage**

In summer the sun is up nearly all day.

The light makes people want to get out and play.

B is for **Bear**

Brown, black, and polar bears call Alaska home.

From Barrow to Sitka, all over they roam.

C is for **Caribou**

Traveling the tundra in search of their dinners,
If chased they can outrun Olympic sprinters.

D

is for **Denali**

"The High One" soars over 20,000 feet.
In North America, its height can't be beat.

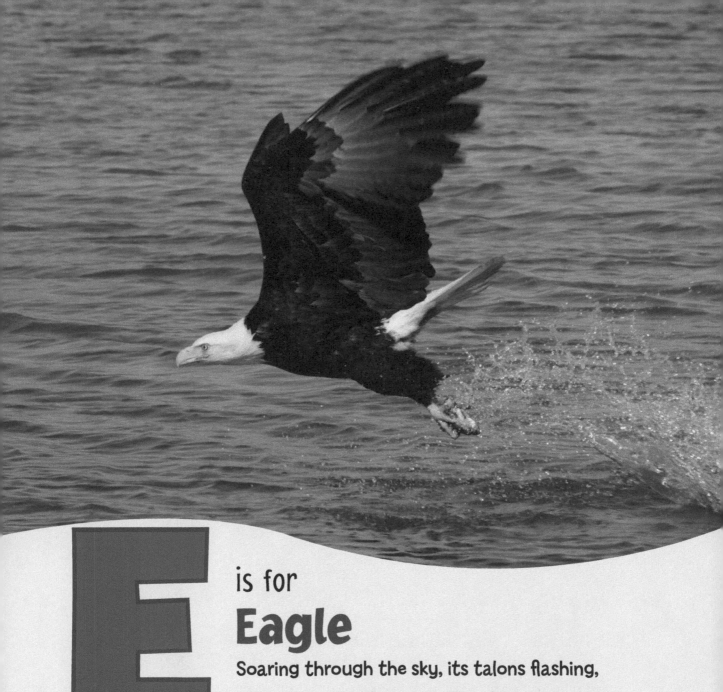

E is for Eagle

Soaring through the sky, its talons flashing,

An eagle snags its prey without ever crashing.

F

is for **Fairbanks**

In summer, flowers bloom
in the "Golden Heart City."
In winter, ice sculptures are
equally pretty.

G is for Gold Rush

To Alaska, many prospectors came.

Most didn't strike it rich, but stayed here just the same.

H

is for **Homestead**

Alaskan homesteaders come from hardy stock.
They build cabins, grow food, and tend to their flocks.

is for **Iditarod**

Each dog team runs at a very fast pace,

From Anchorage to Nome, in "The Last Great Race."

J

is for **Juneau**

Alaska's capital is truly unique.

You can't get there by car when taking a peek.

K is for **Kayak**

Gliding along a stunning shoreline,
Kayaking is a great way to pass time.

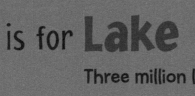

L is for **Lake**

Three million lakes, great for fishing and swimming,

They're also good runways, for planes, water-skimming.

M

is for
Mosquito

Our giant mosquitoes love to
buzz in people's ears.
The unofficial state bird's
been "bugging" us for years.

N is for **Northern Lights**

The aurora borealis is colorful and bright.

You can see it in Alaska, but only at night.

O is for Otter

They float on their backs and eat lots of clams,
But did you know sea otters sometimes hold hands?

562

2967

P is for **Pipeline**

It's vital to Alaska's economy,
Carrying oil to southern refineries.

Q

is for Qiviut

This wool from the musk ox has a
strange name, I know,
But it's softer than cashmere and
keeps you warm in the snow.

R

is for **Raven**

Some in Alaska call these birds "tricksters."

They're smart and crafty, to survive the harsh winters.

S is for **Salmon**

We've got coho, chum, humpbacks, sockeye, and king.
When they migrate upriver, it's a beautiful thing.

T is for Tundra

Across vast and cold plains, many animals roam,
Arctic wolf, fox, and hare all call this their home.

U

is for **Ulu**

This knife is a versatile Native tool,
For skinning and chopping, it's really a jewel.

V is for **Vegetable**

Vegetables here grow huge in the midnight sun.
At the state fair many weigh over a ton!

W is for **Whale**

Beluga, humpback, orca, minke, and gray,
All put on a show that takes your breath away.

X

eXtreme Sports

You can snow-kite, ice climb, or try some BASE jumping. Our eXtreme sports really get your blood pumping!

y

is for **Yup'ik**

Their ancestors came here in waves of migration,
By land or by sea, to this new world location.

Z is for Alaska Zoo

Come see polar bears, moose, and even some camels.
It's home to our state's most popular animals.

Who Knew?

Anchorage

People think of Alaska as being cold and dark year round, but at summer solstice, the longest day of the year, Anchorage actually gets twenty-two hours of daylight! Areas of Alaska farther north get even more daily hours of summer sun. Even on the winter solstice, Anchorage still gets over five hours of daylight.

Bear

Alaska is the only US state that is home to all three species of American bears, and the only US state that has polar bears. Despite their name, black bears come in a variety of shades, even a bluish-white type known as "glacier bears." Unlike their cousins, the brown bears and polar bears, black bears are much smaller and more common—no matter the color of their coats.

Caribou

Caribou actually outnumber people in Alaska (in 2014 that was some 736,000 humans versus 750,000 caribou)! In Europe they are called reindeer, but in America, "reindeer" refers only to domesticated caribou. Even though they are big animals, a caribou can run thirty to fifty miles per hour. In fact, a baby caribou can outrun an Olympic sprinter when it's only one day old!

Denali

Although its official name is Mount McKinley (after the twenty-fifth president, William McKinley), most people in Alaska call it by its indigenous name, *Denali*, meaning "the high one" or "the great one." Since Denali is the highest mountain in the US, the name is appropriate! About 32,000 people have tried to climb it, but only half have succeeded.

Eagle

Bald eagles live only in North America, from Alaska to northern Mexico, and about half of the population is in Alaska. Although both males and females have white heads, female bald eagles are usually 25 percent bigger than males.

Fairbanks

Fairbanks was founded as an accidental trading post by Captain Barnette, who became stranded there on his way farther north. Every March, Fairbanks hosts the World Ice Art Championships, where seventy teams from around the world gather to create amazing ice sculptures. Since winter in Alaska lasts from September to May, this contest serves to welcome spring.

Gold Rush

A gold rush occurred in Alaska in the 1890s, and many of the state's prominent towns were founded around gold rush-era trading posts. Although the rush ended long ago, gold can st be found in Alaska today. You can actually pan for gold at some of the national parks. At the time of the Alaska Gold Ru one in ten "stampeders" were women.

Homestead

We think of homesteading as taking place back in the 1800s, but the Homesteading Act continued in Alaska until 1986. Ev today, some Alaskans choose to live a homesteader's life, buil ing their own cabins and living off the land. You can visit or st overnight in many of the state's historic homesteading cabin

Iditarod

In 1925, a relay of mushers and dogs transported medicine from Anchorage to Nome to help stop a diphtheria epidemic. The Iditarod was created in 1973 to help keep the history of mushing alive in Alaska by running an epic race. The closest contest was in 1978, when two sleds crossed the finish line at the same time and the winner was decided by which dog's n crossed first. Dick Mackey's team won by a whisker.

Facts about th

Juneau

There is no road into Juneau, so visitors to the capital have to fly in or take the ferry. In the 1930s and '40s, Juneau's official greeter was Patsy Ann, a local dog who despite being deaf could sense when steamships were coming in, and what port they'd be docking at. A statue of Patsy Ann continues to greet ships arriving in Juneau today.

Kayak

For more than 4,000 years, some of Alaska's indigenous peoples have used sea kayaks, which they covered with sea mammal hides, to hunt seals and walrus. Today, there are many kayaking tours in Alaska, which allow tourists and locals to get to areas of the state that are only accessible by water.

Lake

Over 40 percent of the surface water in the US is in Alaska, as rivers, lakes, creeks, and ponds. Many of Alaska's lakes were formed by glaciers or by snow runoff from the mountains, and can only be reached by air, not by car.

Mosquito

Alaska has thirty-five species of mosquitoes, most of which feed on humans. Although they're definitely pesky, mosquitoes have been around for over 46 million years. And as much as we would love to get rid of them, many Alaskan animals depend on mosquitoes as a food source.

Northern Lights

These lights are also called the aurora borealis after the Roman goddess of the dawn, Aurora. Although scientists are still researching this phenomenon, most believe that the northern lights are caused by energy particles from the sun colliding with the Earth's magnetic field. Fairbanks is one of the best places to see the lights—they are visible there about 200 days of the year!

Otter

Sea otters can dive up to 250 feet to catch clams, mussels, urchins, crabs, and fish. They are very social, often floating together in groups called rafts, and wrapping up in kelp to stay together when they sleep. They usually swim on their backs, and do most everything while floating: eat, groom, even nurse their young. And yes, they really do hold hands!

Pipeline

Built in the 1970s, the Trans-Alaska Pipeline System (or TAPS) carries oil 800 miles from Prudhoe Bay in the North Slope to Valdez, the northernmost ice-free port in Alaska. Over half the pipeline is elevated to protect it from permafrost. Mechanical "pigs" clean the insides of the pipes to keep the oil flowing.

Qiviut

The musk ox has a two-layered coat and qiviut is the soft under-wool beneath the longer outer hair. An adult musk ox can produce four to seven pounds of it each year. Qiviut is stronger and eight times warmer than sheep's wool, softer than even cashmere, and it doesn't shrink in water. It is very expensive, however; a qiviut scarf can cost hundreds of dollars!

Great state of Alaska!

Raven

They're no "bird brains!" Ravens are one of the smartest animals on the planet, right up there with chimpanzees and dolphins. They use tools, play games, and can even mimic human speech better than some parrots. Ravens have been known to imitate wolves or foxes to lure them to a tough carcass, so the ravens can have the leftovers. Tricksters indeed!

Salmon

Every summer, millions of salmon migrate from the ocean to Alaska's streams and rivers to spawn. The state has one of the healthiest populations of salmon in the world—more than 90 percent of wild-caught North American salmon are from Alaska.

Tundra

Did you know that almost half of Alaska is tundra? There are no trees there, because it isn't warm for very long and the ground is too hard for roots to grow deep. But there are plenty of animals. Millions of migrating birds feast on millions of mosquitoes, while caribou, arctic fox, arctic hare, snowy owl, and musk ox make the tundra their permanent home.

Ulu

This is a knife traditionally used by Yup'ik, Inuit, and Unangaˆx (Aleut) women to skin animals, cut hair, and chop food. The ulu was passed down from generation to generation, and it was believed that the owner's knowledge was contained within the blade and would also be passed on.

Vegetable

Thanks to fertile soil and nineteen hours of summer sunlight, Alaska grows some of the biggest veggies in the world! These garden behemoths are celebrated each year at the Alaska State Fair in Palmer. Here are some record holders: a 40-pound broccoli, a 90-pound squash, and a whopping 138-pound cabbage!

Whale

Eight kinds of whales swim the frigid waters of Alaska. In addition to those in the poem, there are also bowhead, right, and blue whales. Blue whales are the largest animals on earth, but belugas are the only whale that can turn their heads. In its lifetime, the gray whale travels over 400,000 miles—that's like going to the moon and back!

eXtreme Sports

From skijoring to scuba diving, Alaska's rugged landscapes make it perfect for many extreme sports. BASE jumpers launch themselves off a fixed object, like a cliff or bridge, and use a parachute to break their fall. It is one of the most deadly sports in the world—forty-three times more dangerous than parachuting out of a plane!

Yup'ik

Alaska is home to more than 100,000 indigenous peoples, including the Athabascan, Eyak, Iñupiat, Haida, Tlingit, Tsimshian, Unangaˆx (Aleut), and Yup'ik cultures. Scientists believe that today's Alaska Natives came from Asia more than 10,000 years ago, either by walking across the now-gone Bering land bridge or by boating across the narrow ocean channel.

Alaska Zoo

For forty years, the Alaska Zoo has been promoting conservation of Arctic species and providing a safe home to orphaned, injured, and captive-born animals. They are especially passionate about making a difference for polar bears, inspiring action and change as these Alaskan animals struggle with thawing sea ice due to climate change.

From left to right: Andrea Conley, Dae'Lon Conley, Sydney West (staff), Taurean Sellers, and Andresia Conley.
Photo courtesy of Lauren Mason.

Thank you everyone at Boys & Girls Clubs Alaska for encouraging your kids to write and enter this contest. Thank you to the dedicated staff and the team at the Northeast Community Center Boys and Girls Club, Lauren Mason and Sydney West, who guided the youth through this process. And most of all, thanks to the kids who wrote such fantastic poetry for this book. **Way to go!**

Boys & Girls Clubs Alaska focuses on providing disadvantaged youth with enriching programs that lead to academic success, healthy lifestyles, and positive character and citizenship. Club youth benefit from a safe, positive environment, supportive relationships with caring adults and mentors, unique educational and career opportunities, and a variety of fun programs that help build an optimistic foundation for the future. To learn more about Boys & Girls Clubs Alaska, visit our website at **www.bgcalaska.org.**

The Authors of *A is for Alaska*:

Andrea Conley (U, J)

Andresia Conley (P, J, Q)

Dae'Lon Conley (R, G)

Haydin Laflamme (H, L, T)

Ryan Laflamme

Essynce McCright

Sydella Reid (H, L, W)

Jaylah Riggins (A, I)

Demetrius Riley (B, D, W)

Taurean Sellers

Kynsey Stapley (M, N, O, X, Z)

Sydney Stapley (F, S)

Kennedy Thomas (K, V)

J'Lonie Wade (E, T, Y)

Kamelia Wade (O, X, Z)

Kok Yat (C, G)

Text © 2015 by WestWinds Press®

All rights reserved. No part of this book may be reproduced or transmitted in any form or by any means, electronic or mechanical, including photocopying, recording, or by any information storage and retrieval system, without written permission of the publisher.

The following photographers hold copyright to their images as indicated:

Roy Corral, **A, U, V, Y**; iStock.com/PhotosbyAndy, **B**; iStock.com/RONSAN4D, **C**; Reinhardt/Dreamstime.com, **D**; iStock.com/Frank Leung, **E**; Patrick J. Endres/AlaskaPhotoGraphics.com, **F**; Tricia Brown, **G, H, M, front cover (top), back cover**; Patrick J. Endres/AlaskaPhotoGraphics.com, **I**; Brad Calkins/Dreamstime.com, **J**; iStock.com/bruceman, **K**; iStock.com/bergsbo, **L**; Karrapavan/Dreamstime.com, **N**; iStock.com/net_fabrix, **O**; Mike Clime/Dreamstime.com, **P**; Steve Kazlowski/DanitaDelimont.com, **Q**; iStock.com/cjmckendry, **R**; iStock.com/sekarb, **S**; iStock.com/JonnyNoTrees, **T**; iStock.com/ChadKruzic, **W**; iStock.com/Adventure_Photo, **X**; Richie Lomba/Dreamstime.com, **Z**; iStock.com/djangosupertramp, **front cover (bottom)**.

Library of Congress Cataloging-in-Publication Data is available
ISBN 9781513261799

Editor: Michelle McCann
Designer: Vicki Knapton

Published by WestWinds Press®
An imprint of

GRAPHIC ARTS
BOOKS®

GraphicArtsBooks.com

Proudly distributed by Ingram Publisher Services

Printed in the U.S.A.

2018 LSI

Part of the growing See-My-State Series, Written by Kids for Kids!

Alaska

Printed in the USA
CPSIA information can be obtained
at www.ICGtesting.com
JSHW072020140824
68134JS00040B/3712